Brilliant Activities for Stretching Gifted and Talented Children

Ashley McCabe Mowat

 Brilliant Publications

Publisher's Information

Brilliant Publications
www.brilliantpublications.co.uk

Sales Office:
BEBC (Brilliant Publications)
Albion Close, Parkstone, Poole, Dorset BH12 3LL UK
Tel: 01202 712910
Fax: 0845 1309300
e-mail: brilliant@bebc.co.uk

Editorial Office:
Unit 10, Sparrow Hall Farm,
Edlesborough, Dunstable, Bedfordshire LU6 2ES
Tel: 01525 222292
Fax: 01525 222720
e-mail: info@brilliantpublications.co.uk
website: www.brilliantpublications.co.uk

Written by Ashley McCabe Mowat
Cover design by David Benham
Illustrated by Kerry Ingham

© Ashley McCabe Mowat 2008
ISBN 978-1-905780-17-4

First published in the UK in 2008
10 9 8 7 6 5 4 3 2 1

Printed in the UK by Lightning Source

About the Author

Ashley McCabe Mowat is a Gifted Educator and Consultant. She grew up in the southern states of America and was a student in the gifted programme from the age of 8. She received a BA in Early Childhood Education, a BA in Elementary Education and studied Psychology at Converse Women's College in South Carolina. Ashley continued her education at Converse, receiving a master's degree in Gifted Education. During this time, Ashley taught in an inner-city school and completed a thesis on Underachieving Gifted Males. She also planned and implemented a curriculum for the top 100 gifted students in her area for the Athena Institute, a summer programme for gifted students.

Ashley moved to England, married, and in 1999 taught Key Stage 1 at Gateway School in Great Missenden, Buckinghamshire. The following year, she piloted a gifted programme in the school, writing and implementing a themed curriculum dealing with issues of the gifted and talented. The programme has been a great success. Ashley has organized Creative and Critical Thinking Workshops at Gateway during the school holidays and taught at various summer programmes for gifted pupils. Ashley teaches at Gateway part-time. She has provided INSET training days for teachers in schools involved with the Excellence in Cities programme and has worked with the National Association for Gifted Children (NAGC) on their website.

Ashley is available to provide INSET training days, and workshops for children. She can be contacted direct via e-mail (amm_gifteded@hotmail.com) or via Brilliant Publications.

Ashley McCabe Mowat

Contents

Contents continued

Introduction

If you are the teacher (or even the parent) of a gifted and talented child, you'll understand the challenges involved in providing the mental stimulation they require. This book helps you to meet these challenges.

Part I reviews theories and concepts relating to creativity, learning and teaching (such as Bloom's Taxonomy), with particular regard to the education of gifted and talented children. Here you'll also find fun, motivating activities demonstrating how you can put the theories and concepts into practice.

Part II provides a selection of whole-class activities that will stretch the gifted and talented child. These are divided into:

- ◆ Quick Warm-ups
- ◆ Brainteasers
- ◆ Maths Mania
- ◆ Longer Whole-class Activities

Further whole-class activities can be found in Ashley McCabe Mowat's first book, *Brilliant Activities for Gifted and Talented Children* (ISBN 978-1-903853-47-7)

Part III, the final and largest section of the book, provides entertaining, open-ended exercises for pupils to complete independently, further stretching their analytical, creative and evaluative skills.

All the activities in Parts II and III are photocopiable. Cut the photocopied sheets along the dotted lines to separate activity cards. We recommend laminating the cards to increase their durability. All the activities require minimal preparation.

While written mainly for exceptional pupils up to the age of 11, this book presents approaches and insights that can apply to virtually any pupil and to any teaching situation.

Logos appear on each activity, indicating whether the task is for the whole class or for individuals, or whether the questions are brainteasers or more maths orientated.

Whole class

Individual

Maths Mania

Brainteasers

What is Bloom's Taxonomy?

Bloom's Taxonomy is, quite simply, a classification of levels of intellectual behaviour important in learning. Bloom's model describes six levels of thinking, arranging these sequentially from the least complex to the most complex. These are:

1.   **Knowledge** – simple recall. Pupils can say that they 'know' something if they can recall it, recite it or write it down.

2.   **Comprehension** – pupils can restate what they 'know' in their own words. Retelling a story, stating the main idea or translating from another language are several ways in which pupils can demonstrate that they 'comprehend' or understand what they have learned.

3.   **Application** – pupils can apply what they have learned from one context to another. For example, they may be required to decide when to apply mathematical concepts to real-life situations.

4.   **Analysis** – pupils can understand the attributes of something so that its component parts may be studied separately and in relation to one another. Asking pupils to compare and contrast, categorize and/or recognize inferences, opinions or motives would give them experience in analysis.

5.   **Synthesis** – requires pupils to create a novel or original thought, idea or product. All of the activities we call 'creative thinking' give pupils experience with synthesis. Also, when pupils can take bits and pieces of several theories or combine ideas from different sources to create an original perspective or idea, they are thinking at a synthesis level.

6.   **Evaluation** – pupils can judge what they have analysed.

Sample activities based on each of the six levels of Bloom's Taxonomy could resemble the following:

Knowledge   Make a timeline of some of the important events in the history of the world.

Comprehension   Write a brief outline of some of the changes that have taken place in your lifetime.

Application   Illustrate one of these changes in a cartoon strip.

Bloom's Taxonomy (continued)

Analysis   Design a questionnaire to collect data about what people expect of the future. Analyse and present your findings to your parents or your class.

Synthesis   Design a school of the future that would really appeal to children. Sketch some of your ideas on paper.

Evaluation   Select three major problems facing the world today. What are your solutions to each of those problems?

Emphasizing the Three Highest Levels of Bloom's Taxonomy

Most school curricula are written to include only the first three levels of Bloom's Taxonomy. To challenge pupils more fully, and help to meet the needs of the gifted and talented pupils in your classroom, try giving more attention to the three highest levels of Bloom's Taxonomy – Analysis, Synthesis and Evaluation.

To aid you, here are three sets of lists, with a set for each of the three highest levels. Each set consists of useful verbs, sample questions for pupils and suggestions for classroom activities. These can be used when doing short- and medium-term planning to ensure that you have sufficient activities to stretch the gifted and talented pupils.

Analysis

Useful verbs	Sample question stems	Potential activities and products
Advertise	If ... had happened, what might the ending have been?	Write an advert to sell a new product
Analyse	Which events could have happened?	Design a questionnaire to gather information
Categorize	How was this similar to ... ?	Conduct an investigation to produce information to support a view
Compare	What was the underlying theme of ... ?	Make a flow chart to show the critical stages
Contrast	What do you see as other possible information?	Construct a graph to illustrate selected outcomes
Distinguish	Why did ... changes occur?	Make a jigsaw puzzle showing a detailed pattern
Examine	Can you compare your ... with that presented in ... ?	Make a family tree showing relationships
Explain	Can you explain what must have happened?	Put on a play about the area of study
Identify	How is ... similar to ... ?	Write a biography of the subject of study
Illustrate	Can you distinguish between ... ?	Arrange a party. Make all the arrangements and record all of the steps needed
Investigate	What are some of the motives behind ... ?	Review a work of art in terms of form, colour and texture

Synthesis

Useful verbs	Sample question stems	Potential activities and products
Compose	Can you see a possible solution to ... ?	Create a new product. Give it a name and plan a marketing campaign
Construct	What would happen if ... ?	Design a CD, book or magazine cover for ...
Create	Can you design a ... to ... ?	Invent a machine to do a specific task
Design	How many ways can you code and write material?	Make up a new language using code
Devise	Can you develop a proposal that would ... ?	Compose a rhyme or put new words to a known melody
Imagine	Can you create new and unusual uses for ... ?	Sell an idea
Invent	Why not compose a song about ... ?	Design a building to house your study
Plan	Why don't you devise your own way to deal with ... ?	Write a television show, play, puppet show, role play, song or pantomime about ...
Predict	If you had access to all resources, how would you deal with ... ?	Write about your feelings in relation to ...
Propose	Can you write a new recipe for a tasty dish?	Devise a way to ...

Evaluation

Useful verbs	Sample question stems	Potential activities and products
Argue	Are you a ... person?	Make a list of pros and cons
Assess	How effective are ... ?	When you are punished, in what ways do you make changes to your behaviour? Do you think that your parent or guardian is fair?
Choose	Can you defend your position about ... ?	Make a booklet about five rules that you see as important. Convince others of your views
Debate	What changes to ... would you recommend?	Write a half-yearly report
Decide	Do you think ... is a good or a bad thing?	Form a panel to discuss views, eg 'Learning at school'
Judge	Is there a better solution to ... ?	Prepare a list of criteria to judge a ... show. Indicate priority and ratings
Justify	How would you have handled ... ?	Write a letter to ... advising on changes needed at ...
Recommend	How would you feel if ... ?	Prepare a list of activities you would like to see added to your school timetable
Select	Judge the value of ...	Conduct a debate about an issue of special interest
Verify	Do you believe ... ?	Prepare a case to present your view about ...

The Torrance Tests of Creative Thinking

E Paul Torrance, a renowned professor of educational psychology, was among the first to recognize creativity as being part of intellect. As such, he invented the Torrance Tests of Creative Thinking, which have since become accepted as the benchmark method for measuring creativity and have served as the basis for all subsequent research on the subject. The tests comprise two parts: the verbal and the figural. The verbal test requires the pupil to invent uses for common things, such as a soft toy (eg 'How would you make this a better toy?'). Pupils' responses are then assessed for originality, fluency (number of responses), flexibility (number of different categories) and elaboration. The figural test calls on the pupil to incorporate simple shapes into more complete pictures. Responses are then judged on many of the same criteria used in the verbal test, along with the additional criteria of humour and emotionality.

Torrance's tests not only helped to debunk the belief that IQ tests alone were the best measure of a person's real intelligence, they also raised awareness of the value of creative abilities, which in turn led to the development of gifted programmes throughout the world.

Incorporating Creative Thinking Processes into the Classroom Curriculum

Based on Torrance's four criteria of Fluency, Flexibility, Originality and Elaboration, we as teachers can strive to enhance and develop the creative talents of gifted and non-gifted pupils alike. On the next few pages, we expand on these four criteria, and offer classroom activities based thereon.

Fluency

Fluent thinking is the ability to produce a large quantity of creative ideas and thoughts. Fluency activities may ask the learner to generate answers to questions of how many, what kinds etc. Fluent thinkers produce lots of ideas.

Fluency tasks cause a search through the learner's private collection or storehouse of knowledge and experiences for all possible responses. Brainstorming in small groups promotes fluency, as one person's idea triggers more responses from other members of the group. It's important in fluency exercises to withhold all judgements of right or wrong and appropriate or inappropriate, because attention is placed on quantity rather than the quality of the responses. This allows for an uninterrupted flow of thoughts and ideas and a search for all possibilities. The more responses produced, the greater the likelihood of producing an original idea or a satisfactory solution. If you have 20 ideas to choose from, you have a greater probability of having a quality idea within that group than if you have only two ideas.

A teacher encourages fluent thinking every time he or she asks:

1.   How many _____ can you think of?

2.   In what ways might we _____?

3.   What are all the ways you could _____?

4.   Make a long list of things that _____.

5.   How many different examples (reasons, solutions etc) can you think of?

6.   How many ways can you think of to _____?

7.   What are all the things that are _____?

8.   What comes to mind when you think of _____?

9.   How long a list can you make?

Tasks to Encourage Fluency

These activities are great for brainstorming and mind-mapping (a mind map is a written representation of words, ideas or other items connected to and arranged around a central key word or idea).

Make a long list of:
- Ways to get from one place to another
- Things you can catch
- Things you could say or do to thank another person
- Words that mean 'watch'
- Things that crash
- Reasons not to smoke
- Names for an ice-cream shop
- Things to do with a potato
- Things that are soft but strong
- Titles for a television show about your school
- Ways to save paper
- Examples of animals helping people
- Names for a class or school newsletter
- Things that close
- Words that could create a mood of excitement
- Things underground
- Things that have bumps on them
- Things that are symmetrical
- Ways to hold things together
- Everything that comes to mind when you think of a dozen
- Excuses for not doing homework
- Uses for a single wheel
- Invisible things
- Ways to save energy
- Ways to be kind to someone
- Uses for a pile of cardboard
- Titles for a book about magnets
- Ways to make spelling fun
- Things that mean love
- Things that melt
- Things to do with a rubber raft
- Words that make you think of fun
- Things that sparkle
- Things that have a cord

Flexibility

Flexible thinking extends fluent thinking. Flexibility results in many different kinds of ideas. It is the ability to look at things from different angles and to see the situation from several perspectives. It is the ability to shift trains of thought and produce a variety of ideas. The flexible thinker produces original ideas by forcing associations not usually thought of in a given context. The flexible thinker responds well to the questions 'What else is possible?' or 'What is another way of looking at this?'

For example, if asked in what ways an empty paper towel tube could be used, a flexible thinker might suggest using it as a measure for spaghetti or as a tunnel for ants. When asked what one dangling earring could be used for, the flexible thinker might suggest using it as a chandelier in a doll's house or as a fishing lure. The flexible thinker will be able to produce a variety of ideas. From this ability to see things from many different angles comes the ability to produce a larger quantity of ideas (fluency) and more unique ideas (originality).

The purpose of flexible thinking is to generate and promote responses that deviate from normal thought patterns. Flexibility allows for invention and the discovery of new or untested ideas. Flexible thinkers see things in different ways and can find uses for almost anything. This shift in direction and perspective comes through the breaking of mindsets, which is the brave domain of the flexible thinker.

Questions to encourage flexible thinking include:

1. Can you think of a different way to _____?
2. What else might be happening?
3. What other things are possible?
4. What are some different ways to look at this?
5. How would _____ look at this?
6. What are some different reasons for _____?
7. What if _____?
8. What ideas can you get about _____ by thinking about _____?
9. _____ is to _____ as _____ is to _____. (Form an analogy.)
10. What else could you use _____ for?
11. What relationship can you think of between _____ and _____?
12. In what ways are the following two unlike objects alike?

Tasks to Encourage Flexibility

1.   Which would you rather be? Why?

   - A piano or a telephone?
   - A tree or a diamond?
   - A race car or a river?
   - A computer or a painting?

2.   Think of the ways the following unlike things are alike.

   - A banana and a snake
   - A chair and a tree
   - A teacup and a telephone
   - A pencil and a plant

3.   Write six sentences using the word 'spring' in different ways.

4.   Make a shape that is strong, a shape that is weak, a shape that is happy, a shape that is sad, a shape that is angry and a shape that is contented.

5.   How might these people view the word 'charge' differently?

   - A teenager
   - A rock star
   - An electrician
   - A ticket agent
   - A criminal
   - A knight

   Can you think of other contexts for this word?

6.   Describe how a pelt could be seen by a trapper, a furrier or an animal-rights activist.

7.   If you could go back in time, which period of history would you return to? What do you think that your life would be like?

8.   Make a drawing with no people that shows anger, love or joy.

9.   Choose a fairy tale and rewrite it from another character's perspective.

10.   Discuss traffic from the following perspectives:

       ● Pedestrians
       ● Business owners
       ● Drivers
       ● City planners

11.   List all the things that come to mind when you think of nature. Divide your ideas into two different categories.

12.   What if babies inherited knowledge and were born already knowing everything about their parents? Describe both the good and bad effects.

13.   What if we got all of our nutrition through pills and didn't need food? What might be good about this? What might be bad?

14.   Discuss two different points of view on the following topics:

       ● Traffic accidents
       ● School lunch programmes
       ● Dress codes
       ● Status of refugees

15.   Imagine changing places with a famous person. Whom would you choose? How would your life be different? What risks did that person have to take to get where they are today?

16.   Discuss skateboarding from the perspective of the following people:

       ● Teenager
       ● Headmaster/headmistress
       ● Parent
       ● Manufacturer of skateboards
       ● Doctor

Originality

Originality is the creative-thinking behaviour that produces new or novel responses. Originality is often the by-product of other creative-thinking behaviours. For example, when working through a fluency exercise, some learners will produce ideas not thought of by anyone else. The more ideas that are produced (fluency) and the more that they depart from the norm (flexibility), the better are the chances that there will be original responses. In a flexibility exercise, some learners will produce novel ideas as a result of thinking about the situation from different perspectives. These unique responses are examples of originality.

The most original idea can be the first one generated or it can be the one that comes when learners have pushed for one last response. Original responses might come in tandem with fluent thinking, elaboration, flexibility or perseverance, or possibly in combination with several of these creative-thinking processes. The more teachers stress creativity and divergent thinking, the greater the likelihood of original responses. Pupils will learn to value original thinking when teachers provide activities that facilitate original responses and also accept and recognize original thinking. Since original ideas may be distinct departures from the norms, the instructor must blend tolerance and open-mindedness with the ability to evaluate whether the idea not only stands out from the ordinary, but also meets the stated criteria.

A teacher can encourage pupils to be original by asking, 'What else, or what more?' These questions, designed to promote fluent thinking, let pupils know that we want them to stretch their minds even more. Originality will happen in most classrooms where teachers show that they value original thought.

Other questions and statements to elicit original thinking include:

1. What is a new, original way to _____?
2. How could you make it different?
3. What can you think of that no one else will think of?
4. Can you invent a new _____?
5. How can you change _____ to make _____?
6. How can you combine _____ and _____ to make something new?
7. How can you combine _____ and _____ to solve the problem of _____?
8. Devise a new way to _____.
9. Create an ideal _____ for a _____.

Tasks to Encourage Originality

1.   Invent your own number system.

2.   Create your own recipe for peace.

3.   Design a flow chart that shows the way to lasting friendship.

4.   Make up nonsense words and write interesting definitions for them.

5.   Imagine that you are interviewing a football. Think of original questions to ask, and then make up interesting answers for them.

6.   Design a fashionable outfit for the year 2175.

7.   Invent a new game using cards and dice.

8.   Use word puns to write riddles. For example, what do cats like for dessert? (mice cream)

9.   Draw a maze that has only one solution.

10.   Create a new superhero with unique powers.

11.   Write a limerick about a fairy-tale or nursery-rhyme character.

12.   Design a book jacket for a book that you would like to write.

13.   Create a remedy for greed.

14.   Write your initials on a piece of paper, and then use them to create a picture.

15.   Create your own cartoon.

16.   A simile is a figure of speech involving the comparison of one thing with another of a different kind (eg as hard as nails). Write original similes using 'as strong as', 'as gullible as', 'as fierce as', 'as gentle as' or 'as original as'.

17.   Design a modern-day coach for Cinderella.

18.   Create a conversation between two lockers.

Elaboration

Elaboration is the creative-thinking behaviour that results in adding to or embellishing an idea. It is the ability to add details, fill in the gaps, build groups of related ideas and expand ideas. By adding onto a drawing, a sentence, a thought or a story, the learner is making it a more complete, more interesting finished product. The purpose of elaboration is to expand, stretch or add to the original idea.

Elaboration is a creative-thinking skill because the learner is required to ask more questions and seek more answers than are generally given or to take a simple idea and develop a more complex thought. Pupils elaborate when they change a simple sentence such as 'the dog ran' into a more complex sentence such as 'The mangy brown dog ran quickly away from the mischievous group of young boys.' It is elaboration (and originality) when a simple doodle is made from letters or lines. The more the learner elaborates on the original drawing, the more complex and creative the doodle becomes.

The teacher encourages pupils to elaborate every time he or she asks questions such as:

- What else can you tell me about?
- Can you be more descriptive?
- What can you add to make it more interesting or complete?
- Using these guidelines, what can you develop?
- Using these basic elements, what can you create?
- How can you complete this?
- What could be added to _____ to improve it?
- What new ideas can you add?
- Can you add supportive information?

Tasks to Encourage Elaboration

1.   Add details to make a basic drawing more interesting.

2.   Add phrases to make short sentences more descriptive.

3.   Give your opinion on a particular topic. Add information to support your opinion.

4.   The invention of _____ changed people's lives. Explain how. Give examples.

5.   Print your first, middle and last names on different lines, one below the other, on a sheet of paper. Make a crossword puzzle by adding words that describe you.

6.   Choose a children's game and add ideas that will make it more fun or challenging.

7.   Complete this sentence: 'Doubts, like fear … '. Elaborate on your idea by writing a poem about doubts.

8.   Choose a theme for a party. Plan a party around that theme. Include details such as invitations, decorations, table settings, entertainment and prizes.

9.   Given the outline of a mountain range, draw in details to bring the scene to life.

10.   Given a basic car design, what options would you add to make a super luxury car?

11.   List words that describe summer, then write a poem about summer.

12.   Give examples to explain the saying 'Every cloud has a silver lining.'

13.   Given a basic recipe, add ingredients that will make it taste even better.

14.   What things could be added to improve a school bus or adapt it to another use?

15.   Write another verse for a poem or nursery rhyme.

16.   If you could make any additions you wanted to your house or garden, what would you add?

17.   List three adjectives that describe a friend. Use them to write a paragraph about this friend.

18.   Cut a 2-inch square out of a magazine picture and glue it to a sheet of paper. Exchange papers with a partner. Complete the picture you were given by adding details that extend the picture.

19.   Write another chapter for a favourite book.

Brainstorming

What is Brainstorming?

Brainstorming is a group creativity technique designed to generate a large number of ideas for the solution of a problem. It has added benefits, too, such as improving morale and encouraging a spirit of co-operation among group members.

There are some important rules for brainstorming:

1. Quantity is important

Get as many ideas as you can down on paper or on the board. It is not important what you say at this stage; just make sure that you have a long list! Encourage the children to have a 'mindshower' for one minute when they have run out of ideas. This encourages them to think as much as they can for one minute to try to create a few more ideas to write down. (Challenge them to think of 10 more ideas!)

2. No judgement

Don't make fun of anyone's ideas, even your own. Welcome all ideas and write them down on your list. You will have a chance to judge your ideas at a later stage.

3. Accept far-out ideas

Ideas that seem silly are great! They stimulate creativity and may lead to an idea that does not seem so silly later. Good ideas sometimes stem from crazy ideas!

4. Bouncing ideas off one another is definitely allowed

When you hear someone else's ideas, it makes a light switch on in your brain that gives you a different idea. This is bouncing ideas off one another. Just one idea can lead to another, and another and another! Sometimes the best ideas are stimulated from hearing a great idea from your friend.

Brainstorming Tasks

Like all good thinkers, one must not settle for just one or two solutions to a problem. Many alternatives must be considered before the best solution is found. Here are some exercises that you can try (on your own or as part of a classroom activity) to practise your brainstorming abilities.

1.   Come up with as many unusual uses for each thing as you can (aim for at least 10). Remember to have a mindshower when you run out of ideas!

- A paper clip
- A balloon
- A paper bag
- A jar with a lid
- A shoelace
- An elastic band

2.   Use the list of problems below to practise brainstorming for solutions. Come up with as many different solutions to each problem as you can.

- Keep an egg from breaking during a space launch
- Find an invisible person
- Contact home from a foreign city without using a telephone, postal service or the Internet
- Apply paint to a ball
- Heat a meal in a lifeboat
- Warn a person on a distant mountaintop of danger

3.   Get into the habit of looking at things in different ways. For example, consider the figure of a square with a triangle on top. What is it? Is it a triangle sitting on top of a square? Or a house without a chimney? Or an envelope? List as many different answers as you can to the question 'What is it?' Then share your list with a partner and see if he or she can come up with some other alternatives.

4.   Generate alternatives by asking yourself questions beginning with 'What if … ?' or 'What is … ?' Then brainstorm alternatives before settling on a solution to the problem.

'What if … ?' This is often the question that gets many creative thinkers started. Pupils can tackle this question by combining fanciful possibilities with logical thinking. Pupils are asked to predict the implications and consequences of slightly absurd hypothetical situations in order to stimulate both processes. The willingness to risk being seen as absurd is often necessary to find a new idea or possibility.

'What if … ?'

- We had only one meal per week?
- All girls in the future were destined to be at least two metres tall?
- Everyone with the same name had to work together?
- The insect population grew to uncontrollable levels?
- Our clothes were edible?
- We could choose our parents?
- The prime minister was chosen on acting ability?
- You had time coupons to spend instead of money?
- The colour green was removed from our environment?
- Tap water was the most expensive drink?

'What is … ?' Here, give pupils names of items that they have never encountered before, and ask them to creatively but rationally describe what they are and what they might be used for. Again, pupils need to take the risk of being seen by their classmates as 'foolish'.

What is … ?

- A quandong?
- A thinking wall?
- A transit lane in a shop?
- A bouznik?
- A shrimmel?
- A knurler?
- An aquaresponder?
- A virtual graveyard?
- A grand feather?
- A yig?

Scamper Your Way to Creative Thinking

What is SCAMPER?

The SCAMPER technique was developed by Bob Eberle, a US educational administrator and a prolific writer on creativity for children and for teachers. SCAMPER is an acronym for idea-spurring verbs to improve objects or generate ideas. The letters represent the words 'substitute', 'combine', 'adapt', 'modify'/'magnify'/'minimize', 'put to other uses', 'eliminate'/'elaborate' and 'rearrange'/'reverse'. Questions associated with these verbs, as well as examples of recent inventions that illustrate them, are listed in the table on page 26.

After making children aware of these verbs and how they have been applied to existing objects and products, encourage them to use the SCAMPER verbs to identify new solutions to a problem. For example, a young child looking for a solution for keeping squirrels from eating out of a bird feeder thought of eliminating the pole entirely by attaching the bird feeder to balloons filled with helium, which would enable the feeder to float approximately four feet off the ground.

Scamper Task

Combining what you know about Brainstorming and SCAMPER, have pupils brainstorm an idea in ability-based groups. Brainstorm as many ways as possible to _____. The pupils will come up with a long list.

With their group, pupils are to develop criteria to judge which is their best idea. They will circle the best idea and then SCAMPER it. It is important to inform pupils that their idea may not change from the original idea after SCAMPERing it. It is the creative process that is important. For each of the acronyms, pupils will generate ideas that modify or elaborate on their existing idea. At the end of the lesson, pupils can evaluate how SCAMPER has affected the outcome.

On page 27, there is a blank SCAMPER sheet that can be photocopied and used when using the SCAMPER technique in the classroom. I suggest having a laminated SCAMPER sheet and a SCAMPER fill-in sheet for every pupil, that can be wiped clean and used again and again.

S	Substitute	What could you substitute? What might you do instead? What would you do as well (or better)? *Examples:* vegetarian burgers; disposable nappies
C	Combine	What would you combine? What might work well together? What could be brought together? *Example:* musical greeting cards
A	Adapt	What could be adjusted to suit a purpose or condition? How could you make it fit? *Examples:* air fresheners that resemble shells; children's beds that look like race cars
M	Modify	What would happen if you changed the form or quality? *Examples:* parabolic skis; scented crayons
	Magnify	Could you make it larger, greater or stronger? *Examples:* extra-strength medicines; over-sized sports equipment and televisions
	Minimize	Could you make it smaller, lighter or slower? *Examples:* wrist-band televisions; light-weight bicycles
P	Put to other uses	How could you use it for a different purpose? What are some new ways to apply it? What does it suggest? *Examples:* old tyres used for fences, swings and bird feeders; the development of snowboards
E	Eliminate	What could you subtract, take away or do without? *Examples:* sodium-free, fat-free foods; cordless telephones
	Elaborate	How could you expand or elaborate on what is there? *Examples:* a short story rewritten as a play; a simple tune developed for an orchestra to play
R	Rearrange Reverse	What would you have if you reversed it, or turned it around? Could you change the parts, order or layout? *Example:* reversible clothing

S	Substitute	
C	Combine	
A	Adapt	
M	Modify Magnify Minimize	
P	Put to other uses	
E	Eliminate Elaborate	
R	Rearrange Reverse	

Axe Porridge

Apply the SCAMPER technique to futurize this tale to the year 3000, rewriting it accordingly.

An old soldier was once on his way home for his leave. He was tired and hungry. He reached a village and rapped on the door of the first hut. 'Let a traveller in for the night,' he said. The door was opened by an old woman. 'Come in, soldier,' she offered. 'Have you a bite of food for a hungry man, good dame?' the soldier asked. Now the old woman had plenty of everything, but she was stingy and pretended to be very poor. 'Ah, me, I've had nothing to eat myself today, dear heart; there is nothing in the house,' she wailed.

'Well, if you've nothing, you've nothing,' the soldier said. Then, noticing an axe without a handle under the bench, he said, 'If there is nothing else, we could make porridge out of that axe.'

The old woman raised both hands in astonishment. 'Axe porridge? Who ever heard the like?'

'I'll show you how to make it. Just give me a pot.'

The old woman brought a pot, and the soldier washed the axe, put it in the pot, and, filling the pot with water, placed it on the fire. The soldier got out a spoon and stirred the water and then tasted it.

'It'll be ready soon,' he said. 'A pity there's no salt.'

'Oh, I have salt. Here, take some.'

The soldier put some salt in the pot and then tried the water again.

'If we could just add a handful of wheat to it,' he said.

The old woman brought a small bag of wheat from the larder.

'Here, add as much as you need,' said she.

The soldier went on with his cooking, stirring the meal from time to time and tasting it. And the old woman watched, and could not tear her eyes away.

'Oh, how tasty this porridge is!' the soldier said, trying a spoonful. 'With a bit of butter, there would be nothing more delicious.'

The old woman found some butter too, and they buttered the porridge.

'Now get a spoon, good dame, and let us eat!' the soldier said.

They began eating the porridge and praising it.

'I never thought axe porridge could taste so good!' the old woman marvelled. And the soldier ate, and laughed up his sleeve.

Ideas

S	Could you SUBSTITUTE a laser for an axe?
C	Could you COMBINE your knowledge of space and astronomy with your knowledge of the tale? You know that the story takes place in a hut near a village. Where in space might the new setting be located?
A	Could you ADAPT the architecture of the hut to reflect a futuristic type of residence?
M	Could you MODIFY the narration and dialogue to be reflective of possible speech in the year 3000? (How do you think they would communicate?)
P	Could you add humour to the story by portraying the traveller as a new visitor to the planet who PUTS TO OTHER USES the items in the soup – uses quite different from those the woman knows or understands?
E	What details could you ELABORATE upon at the beginning of the story that would immediately communicate to readers the tale's futuristic setting?
R	Could you REVERSE or REARRANGE key elements in the tale's final scenes to provide a new, humorous twist to the story?

Goldilocks in the Future

Now, try applying the SCAMPER technique to the following situation:

NASA has commissioned you to rewrite 'Goldilocks and the Three Bears' in a manner and style that will be appropriate for children living in a space colony in the year 3085. The main plot and characters should remain the same. A lost girl invades the home of three bears who are away temporarily. All other conditions may be altered to futurize the classic tale. SCAMPER for ideas. The following ideas may help you get started.

S	Could you SUBSTITUTE protein pills for porridge?
C	Could you COMBINE your knowledge of space and astronomy with your knowledge of the tale? You know the story takes place in a wood. Where in space might the new setting be located?
A	Could you ADAPT the architecture of the bears' home to reflect a futuristic type of residence?
M	Could you MODIFY the narration and dialogue to be reflective of possible late 31st-century speech? (How do you think they would communicate?)
P	Could you add humour to the story by portraying Goldilocks as a new visitor to the planet who PUT TO OTHER USES the beds and chairs – uses quite different from those that the bears know or understand?
E	What details could you ELABORATE on at the beginning of the story that would immediately communicate to readers the tale's futuristic setting?
R	Could you REVERSE or REARRANGE key elements in the tale's final scenes to provide a new, humorous twist to the story?

© Ashley McCabe Mowat. **Brilliant Activities for Stretching Gifted and Talented Children**

Blockbusting

When you are stuck on a problem, you can often break your pattern of thinking by blockbusting. Following an entirely different train of thought, you can often get new and different solutions to problems. You must force yourself to think in unusual ways. For instance, you might think smaller or larger, or in opposites or like someone living in another environment.

Blockbusting Tasks

Practise breaking your thinking patterns with the children by using some of these brainteasers:

1. Take 12 pencils and make four attached squares. Change the four squares to seven squares by moving only two pencils.

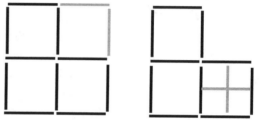

2. Make the following equation correct by moving only one pencil to another place in the following equation: I+II+III=IIII. There are several solutions to this problem.

3. Turn the three pencils into four by moving only one pencil to another position. Breaking a pencil is not allowed. (Answers depend on where the children place their pencils to start with.)

4. Change the pattern from five squares to four squares by moving only two pencils to other positions. You cannot double the pencils or place two pencils side by side.

Making Associations

Creative thinkers often get new ideas by discovering associations between the things they observe around them.

One product + another product = a new idea or product

Try this one for yourself. Select two items from the list below (or think of your own); then write down their differences and find a way to combine the items into an invention that is uniquely useful.

Briefcase	Roller blades	Telephone
Watch	Golf club	Car
Dictionary	Robot	Toothbrush
Comb	Jacket	Radio

One possible invention could combine rollerblades with a watch. What have you got?

Similarities	Differences
They are both for wearing.	You wear rollerblades on your feet and a watch on your wrist.
They both help you get somewhere on time.	One is small and the other is bigger.
They both have stoppers.	A watch beeps and rollerblades don't make any electronic noise.
They can both be the same colour.	A watch has a face and rollerblades do not.
They can both be worn as fashion accessories.	Rollerblades are fast (and hopefully your watch is not!).

Island Fever

You are stranded on an island and you want to get home. There are many trees and you have a saw, some rope, three books, a bag of clothing and enough food to last a week. What will you create?

Pollution Solution

You are worried about pollution. You do not like the way the air often seems heavy and looks dirty. What will you create?

War Works

You feel sad when anyone is hurt. You want to design something for the military that is useful but will not be harmful to people. What will you create?

Sweet Sounds

You like music and think it would be great to invent a new kind of musical instrument. What will you create?

Housing Heaven

You are tired of living in your house. You think that people need some new kind of housing. What materials will you use? What will you create?

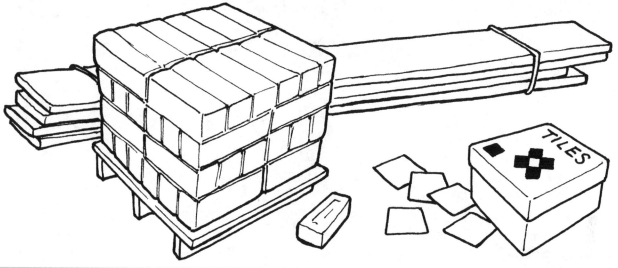

Cook's Delight

You want to make a cake and your stove, oven and fireplace are not working. What will you create?

Busy Machine

You feel that sleep is a waste of time. You would rather be spending the hours doing other things. What will you create?

Clever Cleaner

You see that doing the laundry and housework takes many hours a week. You want to design a fast, inexpensive method of doing these chores. What will you create?

The Walkers' Vans

Mr Walker drove a van with one barrel in the back. Mrs Walker drove another van, exactly the same size, shape, model and mass as her husband's. She had three barrels of the same size and kind as Mr Walker's in her van. Yet when each van was driven onto a scale, Mr Walker's was heavier. Why?

Namesake Double Take

Mr Steven George stepped off the train in France and met a friend he had not seen in years. Beside his friend was a little girl. 'Steven!' shouted the friend. 'How delightful to see you! Did you know that I'm married? This is my daughter.' 'Hello,' said Steven to the little girl, 'What is your name?' 'Same as my mother's,' replied the little girl. 'So you must be Catherine,' said Steven. How did he know?

Whiz Kid Extra!
Extend this brainteaser a step further, writing a story explaining why Catherine was visiting her friend. Give reasons for the daughter being with her as well.

Tyre Trouble

While driving home at 1am, Charlotte realizes that one of her front tyres is flat. Working in the dark, she undoes the four nuts and changes the tyre. But when she reaches for the nuts to fasten the new tyre, she realizes that all of the nuts are lost. She has no hope of finding them. There is no other car on the road. What can you suggest to help Charlotte?

Whiz Kid Extra!

Why was Charlotte driving home at 1am? How many reasons can you think of to explain why her tyre is flat?

Doorway to Paradise

Imagine that when you die, you will find yourself in a room with two doors, one leading to eternal paradise and the other leading to eternal damnation. You can choose which door to walk through, but the trouble is that the doors are unmarked.

Each door has a guard, and you can ask each guard one 'yes' or 'no' question before you make your fateful choice. One of the two guards will always answer truthfully and the other guard will always lie. Unfortunately, there's no way of knowing which guard is which. What question should you ask each of the guards to ensure that you end up in paradise?

Light Bulb

Imagine two rooms, one with three switches and the other with three light bulbs. Each switch controls one of the light bulbs. However, because the light bulbs are in a different room, you can't see which switch controls which light bulb.

Your task is to work out which switch controls which light bulb. You can spend as much time as you like in the room with the light switches, but eventually you must go into the room with the light bulbs. Once you enter the room with the light bulbs, you can't return to the room with the light switches. What's more, after entering the room with the light bulbs, you have only 30 seconds to work out which switch controls which bulb. How do you do it?

Farmer Lloyd

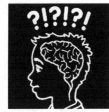

Farmer Lloyd has eight stacks of straw in one corner of a field. In another corner, he has half as many; in the third corner, twice as many. In the fourth corner, there are no stacks. As he piles all the straw together in the middle of the field, one stack blows away in the wind. How many stacks does Farmer Lloyd have?

Galactic Currency (Part 1)

On the planet Xenov, the coins used are 1X, 2X, 5X, 10X, 20X and 50X. A Xenovian has 374X in his squiggly bank. He has the same number of three kinds of coin. How many of each are there and what are they?

Whiz Kid Extra!

Once you've found the answer to that difficult problem, try to design the currency. What do you think the coins would look like on the planet Xenov? Use your knowledge of coins in this country, and in any other countries, to help you. What do most countries put on their coins? Now, what do you think a different planet would put on their coins?

Galactic Currency (Part 2)

As we know, on the planet Xenov, the coins used are 1X, 2X, 5X, 10X, 20X and 50X. A Xenovian has 2349X in his planet bank. He has the same number of five kinds of coins. How many of each are there and what are they?

Highest Number

Look at the chart below. Move up or across from the bottom left-hand 1 to the top right-hand 1. Collect nine numbers and add them together. What is the highest you can score?

1	1	2	1	1
1	2	2	1	2
1	1	1	1	1
1	1	1	2	1
1	1	1	1	2

Magic Formula

Here is a magic formula that you can use to impress your friends. It will enable you to tell how many brothers, how many sisters and how many living grandparents someone has, even if the person is a complete stranger! You try it first.

1. Write down the number of brothers you have.
2. Multiply it by 2.
3. Add 3.
4. Multiply by 5.
5. Add the number of sisters you have.
6. Multiply by 10.
7. Add the number of living grandparents you have.
8. Subtract by 150.
9. Now read out the number that you have.

It should have three digits. The first will be the number of brothers, the second will be sisters and the third will be living grandparents. Remember that if there are no brothers, the first digit will be 0.

What's the Connection?

The numbers in the middle section have some connection with those down the sides. Work out what it is and what should replace the question mark.

3	23	2
1	61	6
7	47	4
5	35	3
9	?	1

Calculator Calamity

Start with a blank screen. What is the least number of buttons you must press to turn the number 289 on a calculator to 17 (without pressing the clear button)?

Magic Square Mystery

Arrange the numbers 20, 22, 24, 26, 28, 30, 32, 34 and 36 in the squares so that the sums for all of the rows, columns and diagonals are 84. Good luck!

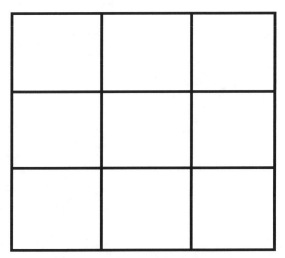

How Old Are You Exactly?

Work out your age in months.

Work out your age in days.

Work out your age in hours.

Work out your age in minutes.

Work out your age in seconds!

Decimal Time

Redesign time on a decimal scale. Make time go decimal, eg 10 hours in a day. Use diagrams to explain how this will work in real-life situations such as school, business and home.

Mysterious Maths

Here is a sequence of numbers. Which number should replace the question mark?

0   1   1   2   3   5   8   13   21   ?

Behind the ?, Part 1

Replace each question mark with either a +, −, x or ÷. Each sign can be used more than once. When the correct ones have been used, the sum will be completed. What are the signs?

2 ? 3 ? 1 = 4

Behind the ?, Part 2

Replace each question mark with either a +, −, x or ÷. Each sign can be used more than once. When the correct ones have been used, the sum will be completed. What are the signs?

4 ? 5 ? 3 ? 8 = 24

Answers (Brainteasers and Maths Mania)

The Walkers' Vans (page 37)
Mrs Walker's barrels were empty!

Namesake Double Take (page 37)
Steven's friend was the girl's mother.

Tyre Trouble (page 38)
Take one nut from each of the rest of the wheels.

Doorway to Paradise (page 38)
Pointing to one of the doors only, ask each guard in turn, 'According to the other guard, does this door lead to paradise?' The answer you get will always be the opposite. So if the guards say that that door does not lead to paradise, you know that it does; if the guards say that that door does lead to paradise, then you know that it does not.

Light Bulb (page 39)
Answer: In the room with the light switches, switch on two of the lights. After 10 minutes, switch one of the lights off and then go into the room with the light bulbs. One of the light bulbs will be on, and two will be off. The one that has recently been turned off will still be hot, while the one that has never been turned on will be cold.

Farmer Lloyd (page 39)
One.

Galactic Currency (Part 1) (page 40)
22 of 2X, 22 of 5X and 22 of 10X coins

Galactic Currency (Part 2) (page 40)
27 of 2X, 27 of 5X, 27 of 10X, 27 of 20X and 27 of 50X coins

Highest Number (page 41)
12

What's the Connection? (page 42)
Answer: The numbers down the sides are placed together in the middle section in reverse order. The question mark should be replaced by the number 19.

Calculator Calamity (page 42)
Answer: 7 (289 ÷ 17 = 17)
Note: Should your calculators have a square root button, then the answer would of course be three.

Magic Square Mystery (page 43)
Answer: Here is just one possible arrangement. Others are possible.

26	24	34
36	28	20
22	32	30

Mysterious maths (page 44)
34. Each number is found by adding together the two previous numbers. It is known as the Fibonacci code.

Behind the ?, Part 1 (page 45)
+ and −

Behind the ?, Part 2 (page 45)
+, ÷ and x

Galactic News

It is the year 3000. You are the editor of the newspaper *Galactic News*.

- What information will you include in the next edition?
- What do people want to know?
- What do you think they need to know?

Remember, a good news article answers the following questions: who, what, when, where, why and how.

Create a major front-page news story for *Galactic News*. Analyse different newspapers of today for content and design layout. Remember what year it is and think about all of the things that would be different! For example, would you have the same problems, or even the same kind of money?

May 3rd 3000

Galactic News

Going out on a limb to keep you up to the eyes in news!

Teacher's note:

This multi-part activity can be done by the whole class, with every pupil taking part and working on their sections as and when they finish their work early. Or pupils make their own newspapers and share them with the class at the end of term. This is a good way to encourage the pupils to complete their task work, so they can have time to work on this project that they will enjoy thoroughly.

Galactic News – Part 2

Advertisements

You are going to add something to your newspaper that every newspaper has: adverts. How do you think newspaper companies make money? They sell the newspapers to the public, of course, but they also sell space to other companies for advertisements. It is your job to think of what kinds of products people would want to buy in the year 3000! What do people need? What do they want? See how many things you can come up with that people would want to buy in the year 3000. You need to make the people want to rush out and buy the products. You can make as many advertisements as you like to add to your newspaper. A few ideas for adverts for the year 3000 might be:

Types of transport
Foods/drinks
Toys for children
Things for the home

Choose your best ideas and design advertisements for them. Start planning your ideas in these boxes.

Galactic News　　　　　　　　　　　　　　**May 3rd 3000**

Get creative and design an advertisement

Galactic News – Part 3

Property

This time, you need to add a section that is a part of every newspaper. Have you ever noticed all of the For Sale signs in front of homes in your area? You see them when you pass the house. However, many people don't live in the area where they are looking to buy. One way for the estate agents to advertise is to include a property section in the newspaper. Look at your local newspaper and check out the homes for sale. Now think of the types of homes that may be for sale in the year 3000. Will they be along main roads? Will they have a place to store transport vehicles? What about a place for eating? Will they need main rooms, and places for sleeping or bathing? You need to think of what will be most important to people living in the future. You can get very creative and design your own types of accommodation. Have fun!

Galactic Property Services

May 3rd 3000

For Sale:
Bargain – Collector's House!
Old-fashioned 3-bed detached
house with garage. Buyer
dismantles. Space needed for

Galactic News – Part 4

Sports

Include a sports page! I know many of you will enjoy this, because you probably play many sports at school. If you were a child in the future, what sports do you think you would be playing? Look back in history to see what sports were being played hundreds of years ago. Were they the same as the sports that we play now? That will help you get ideas for sports that may be played in the future. Use the newspaper sports page for reference. What kind of details does the paper give us? Include all of these in your story. Illustrate and have fun being creative. Who knows? Maybe you will invent a new sport that you and your friends could try.

May 3rd 3000

Galactic Sports News

All the Extra 'T' sports coverage from around the Galaxy by Justaf Maditup

Classifieds and other sections

This is the last section of the *Galaxy Times*. Finish your newspaper by adding lots of classified adverts and other parts that you would like to include to complete your newspaper.

What types of things do you think that people would be interested in buying? Clothes, toys, foods, communication devices or computers? You could think of many things, but remember: the newspaper takes place in the future, not the present!

May 3rd 3000

Galactic Classified Ads

Inside this week

The Future

What do you imagine the future will be like? These questions are about the future in your lifetime. Copy the questions down, answer them and seal the answers in a secret envelope. Ask your mother or father to put the envelope in a special place. Write on the outside: 'Do Not Open Until 30th Birthday' and the year that that will be. Think of this as a written time capsule.

Statements about the future

1. My role in the future is …
2. I believe in luck because …
3. What I look forward to in the future is …
4. At times, I think that we have no control over the future because …
5. What I will do to affect the future is …
6. Change is frightening because …
7. What concerns me most about the future is …
8. My friends think that …
9. If I were a major world leader, I would …
10. A great challenge in my life is …
11. One hundred years from today, we will be able to …
12. I plan to celebrate my 30th birthday by …
13. My opinions of the future are different from others because …
14. If I had the opportunity of living on another planet, I would …
15. The most important characteristics that we will need in the future are …
16. If I could speak to the whole world about something, it would be …
17. I try not to think about …
18. The futurist with whom I would want to spend five minutes is …
19. As a society, it is crucial that we learn to …

Things to Do with Junk

Collect junk from all over the house for a week. Save cereal boxes,
cardboard tubes from toilet roll and kitchen roll, scraps of paper etc.

Select 10 things from your collection.
Make as many of the following things as you can in one hour.

- Something useful for measuring
- Something used for communication
- A trap for a pest
- Something useful in the classroom
- Some kind of shelter
- A container for mud
- A plaything for a small child
- Something that can sail through the air for about 5 metres
- Something that can spin
- Something that represents you
- A musical instrument

Alligator's Dinner

If alligators had cookery books, what would they have in them?

Most famous national recipes use readily-available ingredients. That's why Chinese cookery often features rice, and a traditional British dish would be apple crumble.

What things found in a swamp would an alligator find tasty?

Look at some cookery books, and note how the recipes are written. How are the ingredients measured?

Now imagine what would be in a **swampburger**. Improve the mood of an angry alligator by inventing a swampburger to feed him.

- List the ingredients

- Write cooking instructions (How should it be cooked? For how long?)

- Make serving suggestions (What can be added after cooking?)

The Time Machine

The idea of a machine that enables you to travel backwards and forwards in time first appeared in fiction over 100 years ago in H G Wells' novel, *The Time Machine*. Since then, time machines have featured in many books, films and TV shows, including *Back to the Future* and *Doctor Who*.

Read through the passage below, written by a time traveller.

'Finally, the machine stopped, and a feeling of weightlessness came over me. I have never felt such a gravitational force pull me in so many directions! Impatiently, I leapt out of my machine, but tumbled over in a state of dizziness. The wind was howling and I could hear the sound of crashing waves in the distance. I lifted my head off the gritty sand and looked in awe at this amazing machine that I had spent … who knows how long … inside. It seemed like forever, but, at the same time, only a second. My ears tuned into sounds around me and I heard the familiar sound of a dog barking. Eventually, a human form approached. 'Greetings,' I said, 'for I have travelled a long way to see you!'

What key features would a time machine need? What do you think his or her machine looked like?

Be an inventor and design your own time machine.

Challenge Cupcakes

Have you ever helped someone you know follow a cooking recipe? What did you notice about the recipe? What types of words did it use? Look at a copy of a recipe book. Are there any measurements? How about steps to make the food?

Your challenge is to make up your own recipe, but it will be unlike any of those you will find in a book! However, there will be some similarities. Look at the food listed below, choose one and write a recipe for it. You will need to think creatively! What ingredients would go into these exciting treats? How do they live up to their names?

◆ Challenge cupcakes	◆ Friendship cookies
◆ Value pudding	◆ First-day fudge
◆ Empathy dressing	◆ Togetherness sandwich

Metaphors

Have you ever looked at two things that are nothing alike, yet found something about them that is exactly the same? Once, when I was thinking about a pen and my finger, I thought that they were the same shape. But … that isn't really exciting, is it? I dug a little deeper into my brain and came up with a much more creative way that my finger and pen are alike. They both have liquid in them! Did you think of that? Here is a list of things for you to compare. See if you can come up with at least 10 ways the two things are alike, if not more. You may find that you could go on and on if you really use your brain. Here goes! Get your thinking cap on!

- ◆ How is a biro pen like an underground train?
- ◆ How is a rope knot like a motorway?
- ◆ How are wild flowers like jewellery?
- ◆ How is a mirror like a book?
- ◆ How is snow like the sand in an hourglass?

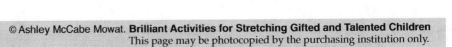

Sound of Happiness

Here are some very strange questions to make you think! See if you can answer them in a really creative way.

What is:
- ◆ the size of friendship?
- ◆ the size of loneliness?
- ◆ the sound of happiness?
- ◆ the sound of sorrow?
- ◆ the weight of a promise fulfilled?
- ◆ the weight of a promise not kept?

Comparisons
- ◆ Which is slower – red or yellow? Why?
- ◆ Which is softer – a memory or a dream? Why?
- ◆ Which is louder – a wink or a frown? Why?
- ◆ Which is funnier – a triangle or a square? Why?

Missing PE Teacher

When you arrived at school today, you could not believe your luck! The PE teacher is not at school and the head teacher has given you the chance to take over! You think about all the games you could play instead of lessons. However, when you arrive at the sports hall, you find that the PE teacher has the key to the equipment cupboard, so the only sports equipment you have to work with is a cricket ball, an orange cone and a rope. Twenty children have shown up and they are getting restless, so you need of think of something really fast.

- ◆ Invent at least five games for 20 participants using a cricket ball, an orange cone and/or a rope. Describe the games and write out the rules for them.
- ◆ If you have had any great ideas, why don't you try them out when you get home? You have become an inventor of games!

Whiz Kid Extra! Make a list of possible reasons why the PE teacher is missing.

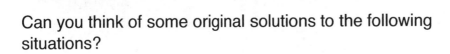

Open the Car!

Can you think of some original solutions to the following situations?

- ◆ Think of a way to open a car door without touching it.
- ◆ Think of at least five ways to use an empty box (apart from to keep things in).
- ◆ Find three ways that these words are alike: little, giant, light.

Give 'em a Hand

Have you ever thought about your hands? You use your hands every day in so many ways, so it is easy to take them for granted.
You have five fingers on each hand (well, four fingers and an opposable thumb, if you want to be exact). What could you do if you had **six** fingers on each hand?

- ◆ List six things you could do with a six-fingered hand.
- ◆ Make a list of good things about having six fingers.
- ◆ Make a list of bad things about having six fingers.
- ◆ On a sheet of drawing paper, trace around your hand, and then add another finger. Above the picture of your hand add the title 'What you can do with six fingers', then write an idea on each finger of the hand.
- ◆ What possible changes would occur in pianos, guitars and other machines or instruments if we had six fingers on each hand?

Whiz Kid Extra! Now try imagining life with **four** fingers!

Wanna Fly Like a Bird?

What kind of changes in our bodies would we need to fly alongside seagulls? How about swimming with whales?

Think of things you would like to do better and things that other species can do that you can't do. Then do the following:

- ◆ Redesign the human body any way you would like.
- ◆ List the advantages of your design.
- ◆ List the disadvantages.

If you would like to find out more interesting things about the human body, do a bit of research. For example, you can:

- ◆ Investigate the armour worn by knights during the Middle Ages. What do you notice about the size?
- ◆ Look into the improvement of athletics records over the years, especially in women's events.

Ferocious Rabbits!

Try to answer the following questions:

- ◆ What would it be like if rabbits were ferocious?
- ◆ What would happen if birthday cakes tasted like mud?
- ◆ What would it be like if houses could talk to humans?
- ◆ What would happen if the Atlantic Ocean dried up?
- ◆ What would it be like if people could see as well as eagles?

I'm Curious

If you are a curious person, answer these questions about curiosity. They will really make you think!

◆ If you didn't have to go to school, what would you do?
◆ What makes the sky seem blue?
◆ What would it be like to live on a boat for a year? List 10 things that would be different.
◆ Where does the fog go?
◆ What do you *not* know about Jack and Jill?

Travel Tips

You can't believe it! You come home from school and open an envelope addressed to you with a letter stating that you have won a month-long, all-expenses-paid trip to an exotic foreign country! As you read the letter more closely, you realize that you have won return aeroplane tickets to the tiny island country of Lamango, and there are no roads (or any cars) on the island. You have also won a month's accommodation at the Grass Hut Hotel, which is eight miles from the airstrip. The only way to reach the hotel from the airstrip is by walking, so you decide to take everything you will need in a backpack.

◆ List everything you could possibly need to live for a month.
◆ Revise the list so that you can fit everything you want to take into a backpack.

Sun Glum

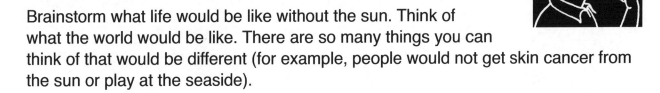

Brainstorm what life would be like without the sun. Think of what the world would be like. There are so many things you can think of that would be different (for example, people would not get skin cancer from the sun or play at the seaside).

What else?

◆ Now write a fictional story about life with no sun.

What's in the School?

You are going to make a list of all the words found inside the name of your school.

For example, if your school was called:

Foster Park Primary School

you could come up with hundreds of words! Here are just a few:

| cool | moss | pot | tool |

◆ Now you try to make a list using your school name.
◆ How many did you find? Try to compete with someone else to think of the most!

Unhang a Coat-hanger

How many uses can you find for a coat-hanger?

You may want to:
- ◆ twist it
- ◆ bend it
- ◆ reshape it
- ◆ or just leave it alone.

List as many uses as you can think of!

- -

Imagine That!

Answer these questions. They are lots of fun!

- ◆ How would your life be different if you lived in Japan? Greece? Mexico?
- ◆ What might be some different kinds of cereal someone who has no teeth could eat?
- ◆ How do you think trees are made into paper?
- ◆ What are 10 questions you would ask the main character in the book you are reading?
- ◆ Can you list five things you don't know about your town or village?

Culinary Utensils

Replace each question mark with a letter to form a word reading across. Then reading down, you will discover that the 'new' letters spell the names of things that are found in the kitchen. What are they?

W	A	?	E	R
D	I	?	T	Y
R	A	?	N	Y
W	E	?	G	E
A	N	?	E	R
K	N	?	A	D

J	U	?	B	O
G	R	?	N	D
P	A	?	E	D
A	R	?	A	Y
A	B	?	V	E
M	O	?	E	D
C	R	?	C	K
R	I	?	E	T
F	R	?	A	K

My Environment

Create a table like the one below, and make a long list of inventions that would improve your environment!

Some things I think need changing	The invention I'll design to do it
Example: dirty air	smokeless factories

Whiz Kid Extra! Can you draw a picture of your favourite invention?

Metaphors

A metaphor makes a comparison between two things. Put on your thinking cap and try to complete the following metaphors in creative ways.

- ◆ Geography is like an aeroplane because …
- ◆ Homework is like a biro pen because …
- ◆ A school is like a garden because …
- ◆ My teacher is like an atlas because … (be nice!)

Make up a few of your own:

- ◆ A house is like a _____ because …
- ◆ A car is like a _____ because …
- ◆ A _____ is like a _____ because …

More Metaphors

Think of creative connections and list as many ideas as you can.

- ◆ How is an apple like a new idea?
  Example: The core provides the seeds for more ideas.

- ◆ How is a school like a factory?
  Example: It works best when we all do our share.

- ◆ How is a paper clip like a dream?

- ◆ How is a worn-out shoe like a young puppy?

Natural Comparisons

In this activity, you will compare yourself to things in nature.

- ◆ Name three ways you are like a tree.

- ◆ Think of different ways you are like each of these things:
    - ❏ a river
    - ❏ a mountain
    - ❏ a meadow
    - ❏ a storm
    - ❏ an ocean
    - ❏ a flower
    - ❏ a drop of rain
    - ❏ a snowflake

- ◆ Listing pairs – what are all the things you can think of that come in pairs? *Example: socks and shoes.*

Stretch Your Imagination

What would it be like if:

- ◆ pizza came out of the tap?
- ◆ the sun were made of chocolate?
- ◆ people couldn't talk, but could only sing?
- ◆ there was a hurricane every year that always destroyed the place where you live?

If I Were ...

If I were in charge of the world, I might …

- ◆ cancel Monday mornings
- ◆ have brighter night lights
- ◆ not have lonely or clean
- ◆ make vegetables taste like chocolate

Imagine you are in charge of the world. What changes will you make?

- ◆ Write down at least 10 things you would change about the world.
- ◆ Write a poem about it.

Xander Paul Dition

Your friend, X P Dition, has been run over by a horde of bulls in Spain during a bullfight! He loves travelling and you knew sooner or later something would happen to him in one of those foreign countries. His leg is broken and he has no insurance for his hospital bill. The Spanish government have kept his passport until he can pay the bill. He has only a few days to come up with 2 000 euros. How can X P Dition come up with the money to pay his debt with a broken leg?

- ◆ Make a list of at least 20 jobs X P can do to earn money with his broken leg.
- ◆ Why is the character in this story called X P Dition?
- ◆ Can you make up more creative names for the character in this story?

Force Fitting Functions

Select three words from the list below and write them on a piece of paper. Next, write a definition for each of the three words.

radar	foresight	document	estimate	leadership	bonus
compress	defend	combine	transfer	elastic	transport
decision	mandate	bloat	dispenser	offer	pitch
jiggle	pack	rinse	add		

Now decide how you could improve a shopping trolley by using all three word functions. For example, the function of a radar is 'radio wave location'. How about designing a radio-wave shopping list inserted into a mechanism on a shopping trolley for locating shopping items?

Point of View (imagine)

Put yourself in the place of one of the following objects. Imagine what life would be like as that object. Imagine how you would feel and what you might think or say (if you could think or speak). Write a paragraph about life from the point of view of the object.

- ◆ Armchair
- ◆ Fountain
- ◆ Old shoe
- ◆ Football
- ◆ Stuffed toy
- ◆ Feather

Design a Cycle

◆ What do a unicorn and a unicycle have in common?
Answer: one horn, one wheel. Uni = 1

◆ What about tripod and triple?
Answer: three legs, three times. Tri = 3

Certain prefixes can tell us much about words. In the 1920s, John Logie Baird invented the forerunner of the modern television. The prefix 'tele' comes from the Greek, meaning 'far off', so it was just a matter of putting a prefix with a root word. Now that you have a better understanding of root words, here is your activity.

◆ Design a cycle for a starfish, spider, centipede or something else with more than two legs. Do some investigation and find out what the cycle would be called using a root word and a prefix.

◆ One idea would be a 'centicycle'. Can you think of something different?

◆ Draw a picture of your invention.

- -

A Better Box

How could you make the standard lunch box better? List ideas for each of the components of a lunch box. Then combine the ideas into a new and improved version.

Shape	Material	Decoration	Handle	Your own idea

Elaboration Tasks

- Find out what an idiom is. Write down a few examples. Now look at the picture. Can you work out the idiom represented by the picture?
- Pick a letter with a tail. Make the tail longer and create an interesting design with the letter.
- Take a small piece of scrap paper and add details to make it into something *interesting!*

Eye Charts

In 1862 the Dutch ophthalmologist Herman Snellen devised an eye chart for testing visual acuity. His chart is still being used today. The chart has eight lines of letters, with the letters getting smaller each line. A person getting their eyes tested needs to stand 20 feet away and read as many of the letters as possible.

- Pretend you are the Chief Market Designer for a well-established manufacturer of T-shirts. You have the great idea of designing an eye chart with a message that could be put on the T-shirts. In order to promote sales and have a popular consumer item, it is extremely important to have a message that would appeal to children.
- Make your design eight lines long, and remember that the letters get smaller on each line.
- Why do you think commonly recognized words are not included on eye charts?

Think Like a Vegetable

Imagine you are your least favourite vegetable. Make a list of arguments to present to other vegetables to convince them to let you into their exclusive 'Good Vegetable Club'.

Improve a Smile

This activity focuses on improving a very basic human event – the smile. By recognizing the things that cause us to see the humour in things, or to feel good about ourselves, we can gain a healthier perspective on ourselves and the events that are attempting to shape our lives.

Smiles are reactions to feelings and events. Sometimes we all laugh at the same event. But because we are individuals, often what is funny or pleasurable to one person may not be to another.

Think of pleasant or funny things that would cause you to smile. Now try the activity below:

- ◆ Brainstorm all the ways you can think of to cause a smile. Be creative!
- ◆ Which three ways would work best for you?

Elephant Day

- ◆ Create a *new* holiday to celebrate something special (not elephants!). Choose the date and explain why it is significant.
- ◆ What traditions would you start?
- ◆ Draw a picture of people celebrating your holiday.

Interesting Sentences

Can you complete these sentences creatively? Try to use your brainstorming techniques and come up with as many answers for each one as possible.

1. The colour of joy is …
2. Being myself is …
3. I feel important when …
4. To be first is …
5. If only …
6. When I am 30 years old, I'll …
7. Mud makes me …
8. Being alone makes me …
9. I am angriest when …
10. I feel happy when …

Reversing Myself

Reversing things can be a means of improving things. To see what you've reversed in yourself, try writing three statements like this on your own piece of paper.

I was _____ , but now I'm _____ .

- ◆ Place a tick by the item you consider to be the greatest improvement.
- ◆ Describe how you made the change.

Now try it with three future statements.

Now I'm _____ , but I'd like to be _____ .

- ◆ Place a tick by the one you consider to be the greatest challenge.
- ◆ Why do you think so?

Hibernation

What would it be like if people hibernated like bears?

Write a paragraph to explain what you think.

Multiple Meanings

Many words have more than one meaning. Think of the different meanings of the words below and write sentences using each word in three different ways.

- ◆ spring
- ◆ hand
- ◆ run

Whiz Kid Extra! How many words can you think of that have more than one meaning? Make a list!

Finding New Ways

- ◆ How could you find the length of your bedroom without using a ruler or tape measure?
- ◆ How could you cook dinner without a stove, oven or microwave?
- ◆ How many ways can you think of to use a blanket other than as a cover?

Sun Living

Imagine that you have the chance to visit the sun! You are the only person talented enough to design a spaceship that will take you there, so you are excited about the opportunity.

- ◆ Draw a picture of the spaceship you will travel in to visit the sun. Consider what special things the vehicle needs.
- ◆ Label the spaceship and describe why it needs the things you have included on it.
- ◆ List 10 words that describe your visit.
- ◆ What risks do you think would be involved if you decided to go on this trip?

Three-toed Sloth

You are going to do a bit of inventive thinking! You may think this sounds silly – but you will just have to use your brain to get you started. I am going to give you a topic to write about, and I would like you to make up a story about it. The story should be creative and inventive. Ready? Here goes:

- ◆ Make up a story about how sloths got their feet with three toes.

Stretch Your Imagination

What would it be like if …

- ◆ ice-cream cones grew on trees?
- ◆ elephants could fly?
- ◆ people couldn't walk, but could only run?
- ◆ it snowed every year on the fourth of August?
- ◆ people were able to jump 20 metres high?

Whiz Kid Extra! Create a sport that uses the ability to jump 20 metres high. Design an advertisement for sports shoes.

Fashion Designer

Do you think fashion will be much different in the future? Use your imagination and knowledge of fashion today to design a fashionable outfit for the year 2075. If you are really clever, you could design a whole collection!

New Shoes

It is often possible to think of improvements for one item by thinking about another item.

What ideas come to mind for changing or improving shoes when you think about each of the following things?

◆ A computer
◆ Peanut butter
◆ A bumble-bee
◆ A Monopoly game
◆ A garden hose
◆ A weed

Write all of your ideas on a piece of paper. Choose your very best idea and illustrate it. You could create an advertisement to market your new shoes.

Grasshopper Alert!

What would it be like if grasshoppers started growing as big as cars?

◆ Design a warning sign to be posted in parks.
◆ Make a list of the advantages of having giant grasshoppers in your back garden.

Invention Categories

For each category, name at least one invention that has been developed in the last 50 years and one invention that you would like to see invented in the next 50 years.

- Engineering
- Food preparation
- Energy
- Transportation
- Communication
- Farming

- Medicine
- Home
- Office
- Recreation/toys
- Personal
- Entertainment

Travel Puzzlers

- How many ways can you think of to travel from one place to another? Brainstorm a long list.
- What is the main method you use to get home from school?
- Survey five people to find out how they travel to school or work each day.
- What changes would you recommend to road rules to prevent traffic accidents?
- Invent a new way you could come to school. Here you can be very creative. Illustrate your idea!

What If?

What would it be like if the moon were made of cheese, and the planets were made of other foods?

- ◆ Make a list of the foods that make up each planet. Explain your choices.
- ◆ Draw a picture of the edible solar system.

The Pet Elecat!

- ◆ Describe a new animal that might become a household pet.
- ◆ Draw a picture and write a paragraph about life with that animal as your pet.

The Spacecraft

What if you discovered an abandoned spacecraft in your back garden?

- ◆ Explain what you would do about the discovery.
- ◆ How did the spacecraft arrive in your back garden?

Be Curious

What would it be like to live on the other side of the world? Find a place that interests you on the side of the globe opposite to where you live, and find out what it would be like.

List at least five facts.

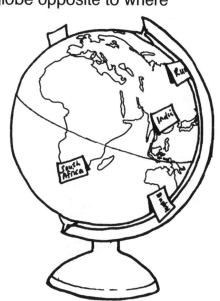

Circle Fun

Try thinking in circles! Use your imagination to draw a picture of a place where everything is round. You may draw a classroom, a bedroom, a playground or another place.

Colour your finished picture. You could do several places and design a poster called 'The Round Town'. Have fun!

Whiz Kid Extra! Try the same activity with other shapes.

- -

New Year's Resolutions

Many people make New Year's resolutions. Think about events that have been in the news over the past year. Think of some people who have been involved in those events. Write a New Year's resolution that will make this a better year for one of those people.

Alternative Uses

Be a creative thinker! Think of other uses for these ordinary objects.

◆ Pencils are usually used for writing. Think of several other things you could do with a pencil.

◆ Soup tins hold soup. Think of several uses for a soup tin besides being used as a container.

◆ Chewing gum is for chewing. Think of several other uses for chewing gum.

A Whale's Tale

The two divisions on the end of a whale's tale are called flukes. Related animals such as dolphins also have flukes. Why do you think flukes are helpful to some water animals?

◆ Draw the shape of a whale's tail. Now incorporate that shape into a drawing having nothing to do with the sea.

◆ Make up a story about a whale that has no flukes. Can you get really creative? Have fun!

Bird's-eye View

What would happen if you were flying a kite and it suddenly took you up above the clouds?

- ◆ Draw a picture of what the place you live in looks like from the sky.
- ◆ Explain how you return to earth.
- ◆ What risks were involved? Could you have been hurt? Did you have to make any difficult decisions? What was the outcome of your decision?

Over the Rainbow

The song 'Somewhere Over the Rainbow' describes what things are like on the other side of a rainbow. Have you ever thought about a land on the other side of a rainbow? Close your eyes and imagine what it would be like. Then open your eyes and draw a picture of the imaginary land you saw with your mind's eye.

Power Challenge

- List as many round things as you can in two minutes.
- List all the possible uses for a metre rule.
- Can you name all the objects with angles in the room you are sitting in?
- List all the objects in your room that are different solid shapes.
  Example: a pencil is a cylinder.
- Group the words that you brainstormed about shapes into as many different categories as you can.
  Example: big and little, smooth and rough, solid and hollow.
- Compare a cube to a sphere. How are they the same? How are they different?
- Why do you think most coins are round? What other shapes could they be? What could the problems be if they were a different shape? What could the benefits be?

Whiz Kid Extra! Think of as many new uses as you can for a 50p piece.

The Unique Seashell

Have you ever admired an abalone shell? If you haven't, have a look on the Internet, and you will probably agree that it is one of the most beautiful shells in the world. The abalone is a large shellfish, found along the coasts of western North America, China and Japan. The abalone, unlike the oyster, has only one shell. The shell's lining of mother-of-pearl makes it appear to be a treasure worth saving. And actually it is saved to be treasured through its use in buttons, ornamentation of musical instruments and many other uses.

- The abalone is a mollusc. A seashell is the hard covering of a sea animal belonging to the mollusc family. How many mollusc shells could you identify? How can you learn more about abalone and other molluscs?
- Think of a brand-new use for the beautiful abalone shell. Describe the product and its uses and draw a sketch of it.

Make a Long List ...

- ◆ Things you could do with old magazines
- ◆ Things with dots
- ◆ Round things smaller than a basketball
- ◆ Things that are warm
- ◆ Things that make crunchy sounds
- ◆ Things that can be cold
- ◆ Ways to be kind to someone

Can you think of a few of your own?

Treasure!

Write down your most valued (non-living) treasure.

- ◆ List three ways science has helped it to be made or to operate.
- ◆ Can you think of a way to improve your treasure? If you can't think of a way to improve it, can you think of a way to protect it?
- ◆ What would you do if you lost your treasure? How would you feel?

Who's the Creature?

What if a creature from another planet came to visit you?

- ◆ Draw a picture of your new friend.
- ◆ Describe a game your friend teaches you to play.
- ◆ Write down the rules of the game and try playing it with a friend. What is the object of the game? How it is different to games you play here on Earth? How is it the same?

Feelings Poem

An interesting way to describe a feeling is by using your senses. Imagine what colour the feeling would be and how it would taste, smell, sound and feel.

For example:

Anger is fiery red.
It tastes like jalapeño peppers stinging my tongue.
It smells like the smouldering embers of a forest fire.
It sounds like dynamite blasting craters in the earth.
It feels like a volcano rumbling inside me.

- ◆ Choose another feeling. Use the format above to write a poem about that feeling.

Drawing Feelings

- ◆ Make a shape that is tenderness.
- ◆ Make a shape that is frustration.

Add more here.

A Creative Puzzle

Pair up with a friend and design a maths puzzle for another pair to solve. Or try making a maths puzzle for one of your parents and see if they can solve it. You will have to be very creative!

Days of the Week

- ◆ Try to find out the origin of the names of the days of the week.
- ◆ Invent new names for the days of the week. Can you give a reason for each of your names?

Tall/Small

- ◆ Imagine you are only 30 centimetres tall. How would your world be different? Can you give 10 specific examples?
- ◆ If you like, you can write a creative story about a day in your life when you are only 30 centimetres tall.
- ◆ Now imagine that you are the opposite – 30 metres tall!

Milk Containers

Milk containers come in different shapes and sizes. For example, in the UK there are several different shapes, sizes and materials (1pt, 2pt, cardboard, plastic, glass). In the USA, milk containers are usually large and fat, because most refrigerators are so large. In the USA milk containers are sometimes used to advertise missing people, because milk is bought by such a wide variety of people (not to mention by so many of them!).

- ◆ Design a new shape for a milk container. What are your reasons for the shape of your design?
- ◆ Are there any issues you feel are so important in the world that you could advertise them on a milk container?
- ◆ Illustrate your design.

No Corners!

What would our houses look like if they had no corners at all?
Can you draw a picture?

Wishes, like Butterflies ...

- ◆ Complete this sentence 'Wishes, like butterflies ... '
- ◆ Plan a party with a dinosaur there. Make sure that you include all the food and entertainment you need for 10 people plus the dinosaur.
- ◆ Draw a rectangle on your paper. Add details to make it into something else. Be creative!

In the Sky

What if you could decide how the stars in the sky were arranged?

- ◆ Draw a picture showing your arrangement of the night sky.
- ◆ Write a message the stars could spell in the night sky.

What if you could visit a crater on the moon?

- ◆ List three possible uses for a crater.
- ◆ Describe how it feels to be on the moon looking at Earth.

Idea Finding

When we have a problem, we have to think of things we might
do to solve it. The more ideas we can think of, the better chance
we have of solving the problem. Look at these two problems and think of some of
the things you might do in each situation. Make a list of at least five things you
could do for each one.

- ◆ I forgot my lunch.
- ◆ I want a toy that costs £3 and I have only £1.

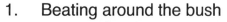

Idiomatic Phrases

Here are a few common idiomatic sayings. Try to draw
them in a literal way.

1. Beating around the bush
2. Cabin fever
3. She cried her eyes out
4. Head over heels in love
5. A bull in a china shop
6. Knocks your socks off
7. Has lost the plot
8. Opening a can of worms
9. He laughed his head off
10. Hitting the nail on the head

Fashionista

◆ Design a hat that would also serve as a handbag.

Falling Star

What if a falling star wrote your name in the sky?

◆ Write a headline for a news story about the event.
◆ Give an explanation for it.

Creative Comparisons

Draw a line from each word on the left to a word on the right.
Then list at least two different ways these two things are alike.

car   pencil

house   telephone

tree   vacuum cleaner

neon sign   daffodil

Make a Long List

What could you roll down?
What could you roll back?
What can change in colour?

Use common points to group objects into three categories. Show the categories in a table. Give a heading for each category.

Read, Read, Read

◆ Write five sentences using the word 'read' in different ways.
◆ Write four different sentences that show anger.
◆ Draw three things that you can do with an old shoe.

Why?

For each situation listed below, give at least five good reasons why this might be happening.

1. Olivia didn't go to school today.
2. Ben's mother is baking banana bread.
3. Sania missed her favourite television programme.
4. Daisy bought some hair dye.
5. Ahmed joined the running team.
6. Jack fell out of the wagon.
7. Lily saw a flash of light.

Coloured Stars

What would it be like if stars gave off different colours?

- ◆ Draw a picture of a star rainbow.
- ◆ Write a poem about the multicoloured stars.

Which One?

- ◆ Which is sharper – a smile or a frown? Why?

- ◆ Which is more colourful – hate or love? Why?

- ◆ Which is colder – the future or the past? Why?

Cheeky Children

◆ When is being good bad?
◆ Find 10 other uses for umbrellas.

Never Never Land

◆ Take a trip to Never Never Land. Write about what you would see.
◆ Be a feather and describe your best adventure.
◆ If you had magic powers, how could you use them to make the world a better place?
◆ If you were making the book you are reading into a film, what special effects would you use to make it more interesting?
◆ How could a magical unicorn solve the problem of _____?

Rhyming Words

The answers to these 10 clues all rhyme. What are they?

1. Reptile or unpleasant person?
2. A dull persistent pain?
3. One way to cook potatoes
4. An implement to use in the garden
5. To rouse from sleep
6. To abandon someone
7. A large body of water
8. To snap a pencil
9. Marker in the ground
10. To falsify

The Stork

For a long time the stork has been a character in folklore and a symbol of a baby's arrival. This tradition probably began when people observed the loving care the stork exhibits to its own young. A stork couple's faithfulness to each other also serves as a symbol for married happiness. They build their nests on and around the roofs and chimneys of people's houses and seek food such as eels, frogs, toads and other small animals in marshes and swamps. In many parts of the world, the stork is a much-respected and highly protected bird.

◆ What lessons can be learned by observing and learning more about the habits of birds such as the stork? Why is it important to protect and study them?

◆ Create a brand-new legend about a stork who became a hero through some act of bravery involving a small child.

What If ... ?

Dragons and unicorns are mythical creatures that have captured our imaginations. Use **your** imagination to think of what it would be like if one of these creatures was real rather than make-believe. Imagine that you have one of the animals for a pet.

- ◆ Draw a picture of your pet.
- ◆ List at least five things that you could do with this unusual pet.
- ◆ Use your ideas to write a story called 'My wonderful, unusual pet'.

A New Planet

What if you could create your own planet?

- ◆ Write three rules visitors must follow when they come to your planet.
- ◆ Where would your planet be in the solar system. Why?
- ◆ Draw a picture of your planet.

Silly Questions

Make a list of questions that:

1. The year 1812 might ask the year 2012.
2. A tiger in the zoo might ask a tiger in the wild.
3. A doctor's stethoscope might ask a disease.

No Shoes – No Problem!

- ◆ What might be some reasons for not wearing shoes?
- ◆ If you were an ant, what would 'small' mean to you?
- ◆ How could you use the idea of pizza to solve the problem of a noisy classroom?
- ◆ How is a teacup like a telephone?
- ◆ If you were a ball, what would playtime mean to you?

Celebration!

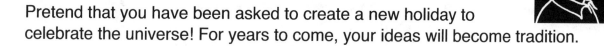

Pretend that you have been asked to create a new holiday to celebrate the universe! For years to come, your ideas will become tradition.

- ◆ Describe a game you play to celebrate stars.
- ◆ Draw some decorations for the celebration.
- ◆ What date will you choose? Why is it significant to the universe?

Parodies

A parody is a literary or musical composition imitating the characteristic style of some other work in a nonsensical manner. Parodies are fun to write, read or sing. An example of a parody of 'The Night Before Christmas' might begin:

Twas the night before All Hallows' Eve
And all through the school
Not a creature was stirring,
Not even a ghoul.
The headmaster's office was locked up tight.
There was just one teacher on duty that night.

Complete this parody, or choose a different song or poem and write a parody of your own.

Body Numbers

Numbers can tell us a lot about body functions. Here are some number facts that people find interesting:

1. An adult body contains 8 pints of blood.
2. Your body is 70% water.
3. The small intestine is 20 feet long and the large intestine is 5 feet long.
4. An eyelash lives for about 150 days before it falls out.
5. Your heart beats about 100,000 times a day.
6. Your brain sends messages at a speed of 240 miles per hour.
7. You have about 120,000 hairs on your head.
8. About 400 gallons of blood flow through your kidneys in one day.

◆ Which of the number facts above is most surprising to you? Why?

◆ How could you use these number facts to help maintain a healthy body?

◆ Write a short thank-you note to your kidneys, a 'wanted' advert for a heart or an apology to your intestines for overeating.

My Own Design

Every year the Post Office issues commemorative stamps. These stamps commemorate a special event, person or group of people. Think of a special event that you would like to commemorate or a group of people you would like to honour, and design a stamp for this occasion or for these people.

Star Formation

What if the night sky made dot-to-dot pictures?

- ◆ Draw a star formation that creates a picture of a house.
- ◆ Draw a star formation that creates a picture of another object.
  Number the stars so that a friend can complete the dot-to-dot puzzle.

Word Play

The way that letters, symbols or words are arranged can suggest longer, complete phrases. For example, you might represent the phrase 'read between the lines' as:

lines read lines   or   llllreadllll

Write or draw a representation for each of the following phrases:

1. scrambled eggs
2. square meal
3. 90-degree angle
4. fat chance
5. double trouble
6. shot in the dark

Think of four more phrases and draw a graphic representation of each phrase. Ask a friend or parent to guess what the drawings represent.

Igloo Living

If you knew you were going to be banished to an igloo for the rest of your life, what five items would you take? (Assume that all the food, water, warm clothes and heaters you would need will already be there.)

Write a paragraph about what you would take and why.

Be Original

- ◆ Create new words for a song you know.
- ◆ Create a conversation between sweet and sour.
- ◆ Invent a new kind of ice cream. Write out the recipe and give it a name.

CPSIA information can be obtained at www.ICGtesting.com
Printed in the USA
BVOC01s1004020215

385597BV00059B/295/P